Workbook Series

WORKING
THE
LEAD

WORKING THE LEAD

by Bill Topp, Editor and Keith Zirbel, Assistant Editor, *Referee* magazine

Graphics and layout by Matt Bowen, Graphic Designer, *Referee* magazine

Printed in the United States of America

ISBN 1-58208-032-1

Table of Contents

Introduction

When heading into a ball game, sometimes you need a quick review.

Working the Lead — Two-Person Mechanics is designed to give you just that. It is the first of two books (the other is *Working the Trail — Two-Person Mechanics*) in a new *Referee* book line called "The Workbook Series." Other workbooks are planned for other sports.

The workbooks dissect details of specific officiating positions and give you an everything-you-ever-wanted-to-know flavor for that position. *Working the Lead* is based on the highly-successful *Referee* book, *Basketball Officials Guidebook for a Crew of Two Officials*. Within its 350-plus pages, the *Guidebook* covers mechanics from A to Z. For *Working the Lead,* we've used some of the best material from the *Guidebook,* plus added more quick tips, articles, graphics and even threw in some advice from top-notch officials — all specific to working the lead position. It compliments the *Guidebook* well.

This workbook will be a must-have for any new official, will serve as excellent meeting and camp and clinic material, and will be a great primer for any veteran heading into the season.

Special thanks to those who helped put this together, including those well-known officials who supplied us with the teaching tips within these pages. Real advice from really successful officials. Credit goes to Keith Zirbel, *Referee* assistant editor and a 10-year high school basketball official, and Matt Bowen, *Referee* publication design manager, for their hard work and creativity.

As with any of our book projects, we want to know what you think. Let us know your thoughts; they shape our future book decisions.

One of the lessons reinforced in this workbook is "stay in your primary," meaning stay focused on a specific task. Do the same with this workbook. Stay focused on what the lead does — and why — and your officiating will improve.

— Bill Topp, *Referee* editor

1 Think 'Lead'

There's a lot to do when you're standing along the endline. Most plays come right at you – and it's your job to get 'em right!

> You must **watch the defense** before judging whether the offensive player or defensive player committed a foul.

> **Think like the offense.** Once you've learned to recognize defenses and understand defensive tendencies, you must think about what the offense is likely to do and adjust accordingly.

> After the shot is released, don't immediately focus your eyes on the rebounding action. **Stay with the shooter** to be sure the shooter returns to the floor.

> Don't Peak. While the excitment in basketball surrounds the ball, **most of the action happens off ball.**

> **Watching what post players do** and how they do it is extremely important.

> Don't let down after a score. **Stay with the players** you watched so intently during the try after the made basket.

> You have to **know how players engaged for rebounding position** *and* how they disengaged.

> **Stay in your primary.** You've got enough to do in your own area, so don't worry about your partner's too.

CHECK LIST

✔ Watch off ball

✔ Be patient

✔ Talk

✔ Get good angles

Bill Agopian, Westchester, Calif., referees the defense.

MESSINA

10 Tips for Being a Great Lead

The only official on the court who has a complete view of the *entire* court is the lead official. The lead's coverage area is smaller than the trail's, but the lead's area has the majority of action. A good night by the lead will lead to smooth contests. Here are 10 tips to being a great lead.

1. Referee the defense. When officiating a game, you must recognize, understand and react to what the defense is doing. Defensive coverages often dictate offensive plays; they also greatly impact your court coverage. By recognizing the defense, you can adjust your coverage and positioning accordingly.

Referee the defense also means primarily watching the defender movements. You must watch the defense before judging whether the offensive player or defensive player committed a foul.

Obviously, referee the defense doesn't mean you can watch only the defender. You must also watch the offensive player for violations and fouls. By maintaining good angles and establishing proper spacing, you can watch both players.

2. Think like the offense. Good students of the game usually make good referees. Why? They have learned as players to recognize defenses and they know what to do to beat those defenses. Good officials do the same thing. Once you've learned to recognize defenses and understand defensive tendencies, you must think about what the offense is likely to do and adjust accordingly. Gaining that knowledge allows you to anticipate correctly and move to get proper angles and spacing.

The more you know about the game, the less chance you have of getting surprised. Studying the rules and mechanics isn't enough. A complete official knows what's going on from the players', coaches' and officials' perspectives.

3. Stay with the shooter. In two-person crews, jump shots from the endline on the lead's side of the court need perfect positioning to see between the shooter and the defender. After the shot is released, don't immediately focus your eyes on the rebounding action. Stay with the shooter to be sure the shooter returns to the floor. If the shooter goes to the floor, know how he or she got there.

Once the shooter has returned to the floor, you can turn to your responsibilities in the lane, but don't turn too quickly. You must be aware if anything happens between the shooter and the defender, even after the shooter has returned to the floor. You must see an exceptionally rough box-out, a poke to the stomach or even a verbal jab and deal with it appropriately.

4. Don't Peak. While the excitement in basketball surrounds the ball, most of the action happens off ball.

Lead officials have to watch off-ball play. Watching what post players do and how they do it is extremely important. While you shouldn't look at the ball until it comes into your coverage area, you need to know where it is on the court. Your position depends on the location of the ball and the players without the ball. If you have "a feel for ball," you don't have to rubber-neck to locate it.

Having a sense of where the ball is at all times helps you be in position and not miss any off-ball action.

5. Don't let down after a score. A shot is attempted, players work for rebounding position and the shot is good. The lead will soon be the new trail. Stay with the players you watched so intently during the try after the made bucket.

The team that just scored is hustling to get back to the other end of the court (unless they're pressing) and the non-scoring team is trying to get the ball and start their offensive possession. That crossing of paths can be a danger zone. You have to know how players engaged for rebounding position *and* how they disen-

REFEREE

gaged. If a player goes to the deck, you must know how the player got there. A scored goal doesn't give you a break from your officiating responsibilities.

6. Stay in your primary. You have an inherent trust from your partner to care of business — business that occurs in your primary. Do it! Your partner will do the same. Call the violations and fouls that are in your primary. If you reach into your partner's area, it not only can create an unhappy partner, it just plain looks bad and leaves players unwatched. You've got enough to do in your own area so don't worry about your partner's too.

7. Let trail have first dibs on a drive down lane opposite the lead. When a drive to the hoop originates on the opposite side of the lead, don't be quick too blow the whistle on an apparent foul.

As the lead, chances are you are watching off-ball. On drives down the lane near the opposite lane line, the lead can't pick up the drive from start to finish. The trail (or center in a three-person crew) saw the entire play and will be able to decide if any contact has created an unfair advantage. As the lead, hold your whistle to allow a foul call to come from the same side as the play. If there is no whistle from the trail and you saw a foul you can call one after giving first shot to your partner. The half-second you wait will not only allow for the trail to call the foul, it will give you a chance to think about the play and determine if a foul is indeed warranted.

QuickTip

Learn about the teams during the pregame

Though there's usually not a lot of pressure on the officials during the pregame warmup, it's not the time to mentally relax. Watch for player and team tendencies while they warmup. For example, if a post player is practicing a move to the basket, take note of which way the player likes to spin toward the basket. If the team is setting many off-ball screens while running their halfcourt offense, remember that during the game. Look for the best shooter; determine if the best ballhandler likes going right or left. Those clues and others will help you anticipate plays and get proper angles during the game.

8. Use your voice. You have two forms of communication while donning the stripes: your whistle and your voice. Use them both.

Let your voice be heard by the players. Keep verbal contact with post players to aid in preventative officiating. Talking to players with, "straight up," "hands" and "space," are ways to "steer" players away from unfair acts. Don't cop out. If you're talking to players and they don't respond to your voice, blow the whistle. If the players don't respond to the whistle to clean-up play, keep blowing it. They will either change their playing style or find themselves on the bench.

9. Use patience during rebounds. Players who have ideal rebounding position (the player has their opponent behind them during a shot) are the ones who most of the time, get the general, run-of-the-mill rebounds. "Wild" rebounds can be hairy for officials.

When the rebound doesn't bounce the typical way, hold the whistle. Once the ball does come within reach of the players, wait and see who gets the ball. If the player who had ideal rebounding position endures contact from behind and still gets the rebound, does a foul need to be called? If you observe contact from behind and because of that contact, the player with ideal rebounding position *doesn't* get the rebound, then a foul is needed. If you hold the whistle, you can judge if the contact justifies a foul. No one likes a "gamous-interuptous" call, a foul on a player who, after slight contact, concedes a rebound to a player in better position. Call the ones that impact play.

10. Move off the endline. Lead officials need to back off the endline to get proper visual perception. You must create spacing on each play that is near the endline. If you're too close or too far, you can't see the play clearly. When you get too close to a play, your view of the play is distorted. Your depth perception is off and your field of vision is narrow.

What's the right distance off the endline for the lead? It depends on your field of vision needs on a particular play. Rarely should the lead be directly on the endline to view a play. Ultimately, you want to be close enough to give the perception you can see the play from where you are and far enough to keep the proper perspective. *(Written by Keith Zirbel, Referee assistant editor.)* □

2 Court Coverage

With a crew of two officials, court coverage is about significant movement — especially by the trail — and making conscious, intelligent sacrifices.

> **The trail's on-ball responsibilities include the area above the free-throw line extended** opposite the trail to the division line and from the free-throw lane line to the sideline on the trail side of the court.

> **When the trail is on-ball, the lead's off-ball responsibilities include the area below the free-throw line extended,** including the lane, out to the free-throw lane line on the trail side of the court.

> **The lead's on-ball responsibilities include the area below the free-throw line extended** and the free-throw lane line (away from the lead) to the sideline nearest the lead.

> **When the lead is on-ball, the trail's off-ball responsibilities include the area above the free-throw line extended** to the division line and the free-throw lane line (nearest the trail) to the sideline nearest the trail.

> **The trail has a much better look on drives to the lane that start on the trail's half of the court** when the lead is on the far side of the court.

> By aggressively penetrating toward the endline when players drive the lane, **the trail can take some of the pressure off the lead** by being in great position to judge the play.

CHECK LIST

✔ Stay wide

✔ Split the drive

✔ Balance the floor

✔ Lead takes pass, trail takes crash

Be ready to switch from lead to trail in the backcourt as Bryan Kersey does here.

DALE GARVEY

Court coverage: Basic Frontcourt Responsibilities (2-1)

In the frontcourt, basic coverage shifts depending on which official is on-ball.

In MechaniGram 2-1, the lead's on-ball responsibilities include the area below the free-throw line extended to the far edge of the free-throw lane line (away from the lead) when the lead is opposite the trail and the floor is balanced.

When the lead is on-ball, the trail's off-ball responsibilities include the area above the free-throw line extended to the division line and the lane area from the free-throw lane line (nearest the trail) to the sideline nearest the trail.

The MechaniGram illustrates basic guidelines for coverage. Specific officiating movements designed to better cover particular plays force the officials to adjust coverage. □

2-1

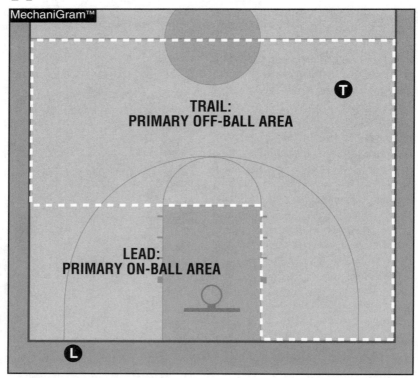

TRAIL:
PRIMARY OFF-BALL AREA

LEAD:
PRIMARY ON-BALL AREA

Boundary Coverage: Basic Frontcourt Responsibilities (2-2)

Covering boundary lines is among the most difficult tasks using a crew of two officials. By correctly placing so much emphasis on off-ball coverage for the lead, some boundary line coverage sometimes gets sacrificed.

The NFHS manual states that in the frontcourt the lead is responsible for the sideline nearest the lead and the endline. The trail is responsible for the division line and the sideline nearest the trail. While in theory that sounds easy, the actual practice is very difficult and sacrifices off-ball coverage in the lane area.

Here's an example. A trouble spot for two-person crews is a player who has the ball near the sideline above the free-throw line extended and opposite the trail. The trail correctly moves toward the center of the court to officiate the action on the player with the ball, such as fouls, traveling violations, etc.

2-2

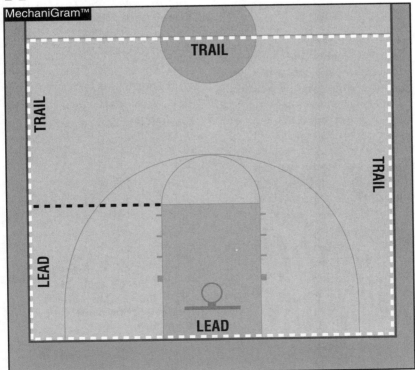

MechaniGram™

TRAIL

TRAIL

TRAIL

LEAD

LEAD

The problem: Manuals state that sideline is the lead's responsibility. Well, if the lead has to look beyond the free-throw line extended to watch for a potential sideline violation and the trail has to watch for fouls, etc., who is watching the other players? No one. There are too many off-ball problems that can occur if no one is supervising those players.

Referee recommends that the trail also have opposite sideline responsibility above the free-throw line extended. Sometimes, the trail must move well beyond the center of the court to see an out-of-bounds violation. Stay deep (toward the division line) on the play to get a good angle.

Though not the best sideline coverage, you're making a conscious sacrifice. You might occasionally miss an out-of-bounds call. Obviously, we don't want to miss calls. However, that's better than missing an off-ball elbow to a player's head because no one was watching. It's a trade-off we must make: Off-ball coverage to control rough physical play is more important than an occasional missed sideline violation. □

Split The Court on Drives to The Basket (2-3)

Sometimes, the lead doesn't have enough time to get ball side, avoid quicksand and get a good look on drives toward the basket. When players make quick passes away from the lead that cover a great distance, it's difficult to react in time to get a good angle.

When that happens, there's a simple solution: "You take the stuff on your side of the hoop and I'll take the stuff on my side of the hoop."

BRIAN SPURLOCK

Try This

"As the lead official, we need to watch the initial setup of the post players. We realize that there's going to be contact, and immediately we have to determine whether it's incidental contact or rough play."

— Ted Hillary
NCAA Division I Men's Official

There's a great myth among referees that the lead is the only official who can call block/charge near the lane. That's wrong. That attitude places too much pressure on the lead because there's too much to watch. It also leaves the lead straightlined and guessing on many plays that aren't on the lead's side of the floor.

When the lead is on the far side of the court, the trail has a much better look on drives to the lane that start on the trail's half of the court. But it takes an aggressive, hard-working trail to make the call correctly and with conviction.

In MechaniGram 2-3, the officials start the play with the floor balanced. ② quickly passes to ①, who quickly passes to ③. ③ immediately drives around ③ toward the basket. The action is too fast for the lead to move ball side. As ③ drives toward the basket, ④ steps in to take a charge. The trail penetrates toward the endline, gets a good angle and makes the judgment on the contact. □

2-3

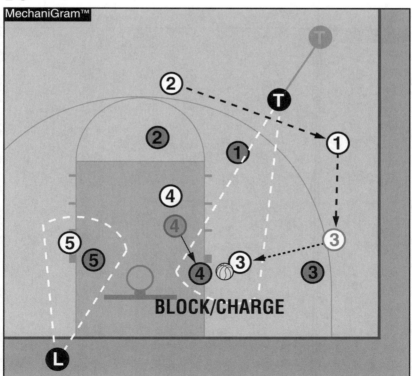

BLOCK/CHARGE

Pass/crash in The Lane (2-4)

A player driving a crowded lane, passing off to a teammate, then crashing into a defender can be one of the most difficult plays to officiate. Why? There's a lot going on in a small area in a short period of time.

For the lead, the play is especially tough to handle alone. Did the passer get fouled? Did the passer foul? Block? Charge? Did the passer foul after releasing the ball or was it a player-control foul? Did the dribbler travel? Did the player filling the lane catch the pass cleanly and travel or did the player merely fumble and recover? Did the violation occur before the foul? Oh, and by the way ... just who is shooting the one-and-one at the other end? That's way too much for one official to handle in most cases.

The trail must help. By aggressively penetrating toward the endline when players drive the lane, the trail can take some of the pressure off the lead by being in great position to judge the play.

The common phrase that sums up responsibilities is, "Lead

2-4

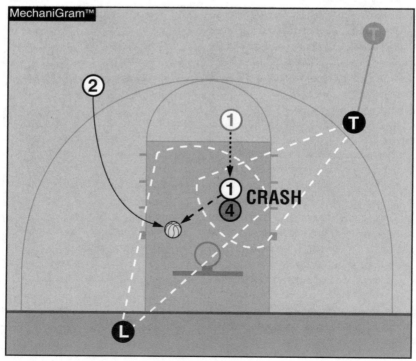

takes the pass, trail takes the crash." That's generally accurate when the pass is toward the lead. However, when the pass is toward the trail (especially out toward the perimeter), the trail should take the pass and the lead take the crash.

The lead can concentrate primarily on the pass toward the lead and the player receiving it. Don't fall into the trap, however, of leaving all crashes to the trail. For the lead, the pass is primary, but the crash is secondary. You'd rather have a call on the crash from the lead than a no-call that lets a foul get away. Be prepared to make a call as the lead if you have to.

If the dribbler passes the ball toward the trail, the trail takes the pass and the lead takes the crash. Be especially wary of dribblers who leave their feet and then make long passes out to the perimeter toward the trail.

In MechaniGram 2-4, ① drives the lane. When ④ steps up to stop the drive, ① passes to ②, who was filling the lane. The trail penetrates toward the endline to get a good angle on the play. The trail has primary coverage on the crash. The lead watches ② catch the pass and lay it in. The lead also has secondary coverage of the crash.

Whatever call is made and whoever makes it, sell it! It's a real "bang-bang" play that can have major implications. □

QuickTip

Angle Shoulders for Better View

A slight shoulder turn will help your view as the lead official.

If you're the lead with on-ball coverage (like in many two-person crew situations), make sure you watch the shooter all the way back to the court. Why? You don't want the shooter fouled on the way down after you've shifted your focus elsewhere.

Sometimes, you also have some rebounding responsibility — a daunting task when you're watching the shooter properly. When you have to watch both, understand your primary responsibility (the shooter) and your secondary responsibility (the rebounders). To help cover both, angle your shoulders slightly toward the basket (as in the PlayPic) to help you watch both areas. Your peripheral vision and sight lines improve.

PlayPic™

Straightlining (2-5)

"Straightlining" occurs when your view of a play is obstructed by the players themselves. In effect, you are in a straight line with the players and have no angle to see between them.

A one- or two-step move left or right eliminates straightlining. Keep your head up and continually watch the play when moving.

The most common straightlining concerns:

1. Offensive player with the ball with defensive pressure. You must avoid straightlining so that you can see between the players and correctly judge the play. Did the defender slap the dribbler's arm? Did the offensive player push off on the drive? Did the defender establish legal guarding position?

2. Low post play. To correctly officiate action around the low blocks — on-ball or off-ball — you must avoid straightlining. Coupled with proper spacing, you can judge whether or not the

2-5A

Straightlined

offensive player pushed off to receive the drop pass, the defender pushed the offensive post player in the lower back or if the offensive player hooked the defender on the spin move to the basket.

3. Screens. Get good angles to see screens. Avoid straightlining and you'll see if the screen was legally set, if the defender fouled while pushing through the screen or if the screener fouled by extended a leg, hip or elbow.

Those decisions and others are nearly impossible if you're straightlined.

PlayPics 2-5A and 2-5B show a play with the official's view. In PlayPic 2-5A, the official is straightlined. In PlayPic 2-5B, the official has a better angle. □

2-5B

Good angle

3 The Lead: Where To Go

You must adjust your positioning to get the best angles. Sacrifice and hustle are paramount.

> The lead must **use ball side mechanics** by anticipating a weak side play and moving across the endline to get an angle on the weak side low-post action.

> The lead will only move ball side when **the perimeter player with the ball is near or below the free-throw line extended.**

> Keep your **head and shoulders turned toward the players** in the lane when moving.

> **Never position yourself** directly under the basket.

> When the ball drops below the free-throw line extended on the lead side of the court, the lead has two responsibilities: **Watch the post players on the near low block and watch the perimeter player with the ball.**

> To improve on-ball coverage, **back off the endline** and move toward the sideline when necessary.

> **Perception is important.** If you look like you're close to the play and in good position, your ruling has a better chance of being accepted.

CHECK LIST

✔ Watch the set up

✔ Anticipate player action

✔ Move to improve

✔ Back off the endline

When on ball, look through the play, as Tracy Black, Indianapolis, does here.

JIM WHITE

Lead Must Use Ball Side Mechanics (3-1)

Many teams today use off-ball screens to free post players near the basket. In the MechaniGram, ⑤ screens ④ so ④ can flash ball side and receive a drop pass from ② . If the play works effectively, the post player is open, catches the ball and scores an easy lay-up. Defensive players will either try to cut off the post player's movement to the open spot or race to challenge the post player's shot.

The lead must anticipate the play (that does not mean anticipate a foul!) and move across the endline to get an angle on the action moving toward the open spot. In MechaniGram 3-1A, the lead official has moved across the endline to clearly see the post player catch the ball and attempt a shot. The lead's in a great position to see the oncoming defensive players and any potential violations or fouls. Generally, the lead will only move ball side when the perimeter player with the ball is near or below the free-throw line extended.

Keep your head and shoulders turned toward the players in the lane when moving. Remember, you still have responsibilities for watching the screen and other action in your primary area. If you

3-1A

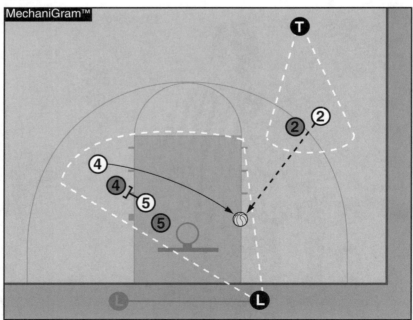

put your head down and sprint across the lane to the new spot, you will miss off-ball contact. Move with dispatch, but move under control and with your eyes on your primary off-ball area. If the ball moves out of the post area, simply move back to your original position to balance the floor with the trail.

The lead moves for two reasons: The lead is in a better position to see the play clearly (if the lead stayed on the off-ball side he would be looking through bodies and guessing) and the lead is closer to the play, which helps sell the call or no-call. Perception is important. If you look like you're close to the play and in good position, your ruling has a better chance of being accepted.

The lead must anticipate a drop pass into the low post on the opposite lane line when the ball is

below the free-throw line extended. In PlayPic 3-1B, the lead is near the lane line opposite the play. It is a terrible angle to watch the post play. The lead is straight-lined.

In PlayPic 3-1C, the lead has moved across the endline to the lane line on the trail side of the court to clearly see the post play. The lead is in a much better position to see potential violations or fouls.

Lead Ball Side: Movement After Made Basket (3-2)

When the lead is ball side watching action in the post and a goal is scored, there's no need to rush back to the lane line opposite the trail and balance the floor. If immediately after the made basket you can balance the floor with-

3-1B

Bad angle

3-1C

Good angle

out interfering with the ensuing play and without missing action around the throw-in area, do so.

However, in most situations there is not enough time to balance the floor without interfering and missing action. If you don't have time to get over, don't panic. You've still got a pretty good angle to watch all the action.

Watch for players interfering with the ball after the made basket. Watch the player collect the ball and move out-of-bounds for the throw-in. Then, watch the thrower, the throw-in and action in the lane area. You can do all that from the lane line on the trail side of the floor.

After the throw-in is made, quickly swing behind the thrower toward the far sideline to balance the floor.

In MechaniGram 3-2A, the lead is ball side watching the post players when ② makes a jump shot. ④ grabs the ball and moves out-of-bounds for a throw-in. The lead does not have enough time to balance the floor before the throw-in. In MechaniGram 3-2B, ④ is out-of-bounds and throws an inbounds pass to ② . The lead, still on the opposite side, watches the thrower and throw-in, then quickly swings behind the thrower to balance the floor. □

3-2A

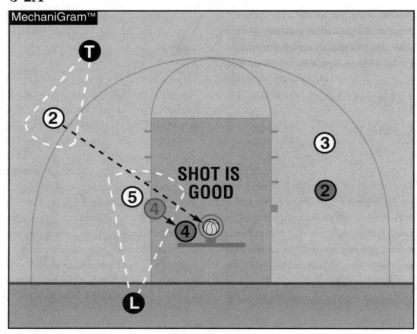

Try This

"The lead is the quarterback, the decision maker, on who works on the ball and off the ball. The lead must have a feel for the game. Knowing the offensive sequence and defense response is important."

— Ed Rush
NBA Director of Officiating

3-2B

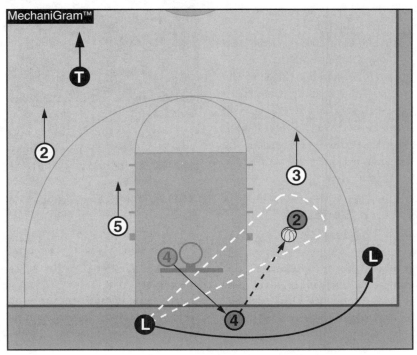

Lead Movement Toward Sideline (3-3)

When the ball drops below the free-throw line extended on the lead side of the court, the lead has two responsibilities: Watch the post players on the near low block and watch the perimeter player with the ball. It is difficult to see both areas.

To give yourself a chance, back off the endline and move toward the sideline. Your shoulders should not be parallel to the endline. Angle them slightly; that movement increases your field of vision and gives you a chance to see both areas.

In PlayPic 3-3A, the lead is too close to the play and is not close enough to the sideline.

In PlayPic 3-3B, the lead is in better position after moving off the endline, moving closer to the sideline and angling the shoulders. Primary coverage is on-ball; secondary coverage is off-ball. With that improved position, the lead has a chance to see both in his field of view.

Proper Spacing For The Lead (3-4)

Lead officials need to back off the endline to give proper visual perception. You must create "spacing" on each play that is near the endline. Spacing is the distance

3-3A

Too close

3-3B

Good angle

between you and the play. If you're too close or too far, you can't see the play clearly.

When you get too close to a play, your view of the play is distorted. Your depth perception is off and your field of vision is narrow.

In most small gyms, the lead's spacing ability is limited. When a wall is close behind you, back up as far as you can without leaning up against the wall. If you still feel there's not enough room, adjust toward the sideline to create more spacing. You might be giving up a great angle, but you're seeing the whole play better.

What's the right distance off the endline for the lead? It depends on your field of vision needs on a particular play. If the play is directly in front of you and you are on-ball, move about five-10 feet off the endline. If the players are away from you and you're off-ball, position yourself about two to five feet off the endline. Rarely should the lead be directly on the endline to view a play. Ultimately, you want to be close enough to give the perception you can see the play from where you are and far enough to keep the proper perspective.

In PlayPic 3-4A, the lead is too close. In PlayPic 3-4B, the lead creates proper spacing by backing up. □

3-4A

Too close

3-4B

Good spacing

Free Throws

Free-throw administration requires teamwork between the lead and the trail. Smooth running free-throw administration looks sharp.

> **Look for late-arriving substitutes** at the scorer's table and beckon them in if appropriate.

> Signal the number of remaining free throws to the players in the lane and the free thrower. Simultaneously **verbalize the number of free throws.**

> Before bouncing the ball to the free thrower, **make sure there are no players moving** into or leaving lane spaces.

> When the free thrower is ready to catch the ball, **bounce the ball** to the free thrower.

> **Move to the appropriate spot** for free-throw coverage.

> After the shot is airborne, **adjust your position** along the end-line a step or two to get a good angle on strong side rebounding.

> For the lead official, **technical-foul administration varies little** from regular free-throw administration.

CHECK LIST

✔ Bounce the ball

✔ Check the table

✔ Look across the lane

✔ Stay off the endline

Check the table before bouncing the ball to the free thrower, as Kim Watt does here.

DALE GARVEY

Free Throw Coverage (4-1)

The lead watches players on the opposite lane line (closer to the trail) for potential violations, etc. The lead also watches the lane space nearest the endline on the lane line nearest the lead.

The positioning means better coverage of the low-block area opposite the trail.

In MechaniGram 4-1, the lead looks opposite and watches ③, ③, ⑤ and ④, plus ⑤ nearest the lead.

As a point of emphasis, you should look for defensive players using hands or arms to disconcert the free thrower. Warn the players to prevent such actions, if you can. If the defender's actions warrant a violation, award a substitute free throw if the charity toss is missed. If that doesn't stop the illegal actions, use the technical foul. □

Free Throw: Lead Movement (4-2)

Before administering the free throw, the lead has the ball and is positioned in the lane under the basket. Look for late-arriving substitutes at the scorer's table and beckon them in if appropriate.

4-1

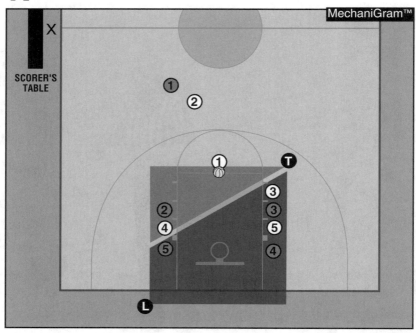

Signal the number of remaining free throws to the players in the lane and the free thrower (PlayPic 4-2A). Simultaneously verbalize the number of free throws. Before bouncing the ball to the free thrower, make sure there are no players moving into or leaving lane spaces.

When the free thrower is ready to catch the ball, bounce the ball to the free thrower (PlayPic 4-2B).

The NFHS manual states that the lead is positioned "approximately four feet from the nearer lane line well off the endline". That position is maintained regardless of the number of free throws.

After the shot is airborne, adjust your position along the endline a step or two to get a good angle on strong side rebounding (PlayPic 4-2C). □

Free Throw: Technical Fouls 4-3

For the lead official, technical-foul administration varies little from regular free-throw administration.

The lead handles the ball, indicates the number of free throws,

4-3

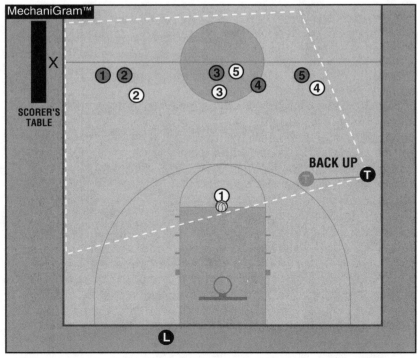

checks the scorer's table for any problems, bounces the ball to the free thrower and moves to a normal free throw coverage position just off the endline.

Keep in mind that your partner will likely step back toward the sideline, as in Mechanigram 4-3, to watch all the players above the free-throw line. You can also keep an eye out for problem from your position along the endline. Don't lose focus on the shooter, but extend your view a bit to help out the trail.

Technical fouls can sometimes get emotional. Don't let it. Treat the technical foul as any other foul call. Make sure that if you're not the one who called it, you help make sure your partner maintains composure. Meet with your partner near the center circle after the technical to make sure both of you are on the same page. Make sure the proper team is shooting the free throws at the proper goal. It's easy to get spun around and shoot at the wrong basket if you're not careful. Take your time; nothing can happen without you. □

BRIAN SPURLOCK

Try This

"One of the most important keys in officiating at any level is communication. If I miss a call on the court and know I missed it, I tell the player and the coach because I think that's important, that's part of being honest."

**— Mike Wood
NCAA Division I Men's Official**

Throw-ins

Proper throw-in administration is critical to ensure your games run smoothly. There are probably more unwanted game interruptions during throw-ins than during any other segment of the game.

> On all throw-ins, the officials **use the boxing-in method.** That means the thrower-in (and likely, most of the players) is always between the two officials; the thrower is "boxed in" for proper court coverage.

> **The lead administers all throw-ins on the frontcourt endline** and along the lead's sideline if below the free-throw line extended.

When the lead administers:

> The thrower is always **between the lead and the thrower's goal.**

> Unless otherwise dictated by an anticipated play, **the lead is positioned on the endline on the opposite side of the court from the trail,** ensuring both sidelines, the frontcourt endline and the division line are covered.

> Hand the ball to the thrower **with the inside hand** (closest to the thrower).

> **Raises the other arm** to give the "start clock" signal to the timer.

> Move away from the thrower to avoid straightlining. Staying too close to the thrower blocks court vision. Take at least **one step laterally away from the thrower** so your field of vision increases.

CHECK LIST

- ✔ Use inside hand
- ✔ Step away
- ✔ Step back
- ✔ Watch the plane

Hand the ball to the thrower with the inside hand, as Jack Thompson, Oklahoma City, Okla., does here.

RANDY BENNET

Throw-in Spots (5-1)

Stoppages of play inside the key circle, plus the area from the free-throw line corners to the endline corners and below, result in throw-ins along the endline nearest the stoppage of play. All throw-ins from the endline shall be outside the free-throw lane lines extended. Stoppages of play outside that area result in throw-ins along the sideline nearest the stoppages.

Be precise with throw-in spots. The ball should be put in play exactly where it went out of play. Many officials incorrectly move the throw-in spot, either out of laziness or ease of administration. Don't fall into that trap; a moved throw-in spot impacts the ensuing throw-in. Most of the time, specific plays are called by coaches based on the location of the throw-in spot. Moving it creates an unfair advantage for one of the teams.

If a throw-in is immediately preceded by a timeout, make sure both officials are aware of the throw-in spot. Coaches will often ask the closest official where the throw-in spot is so the coach can discuss an appropriate play with his players during the timeout. It's awkward at best when the coach asks for the throw-in spot and you don't know. Be ready. □

5-1

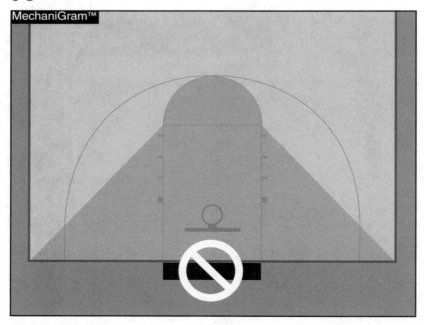

MechaniGram™

Running The Endline (5-2)

If the player may run the endline, tell the thrower that before handing over the ball. Say something like, "You can run it," so the player knows of the option. It's also a good idea to wave your arm in front of you parallel to the endline (similar to a three-second call signal but with your arm swinging parallel to the endline). That shows everyone you've told the player it is not a designated-spot throw-in (again, you'll be seen on video handling it correctly). □

5-2

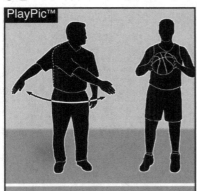

Do Not Break The Plane (5-3)

When a defensive player is guarding the throw-in closely and is positioned very close to the boundary line, use preventive officiating. Before handing the ball to the thrower, tell the defensive player to avoid a violation and not break the plane of the boundary line. It's a good idea to hold your hand up, using a stop sign signal, over the boundary line plane while talking to the player. That shows everyone you've warned the player not to violate (and it's on video). □

5-3

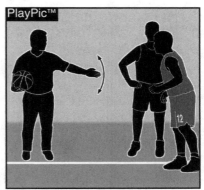

QuickTip

Use Your Whistle Sparingly

There are times when it's a good idea to sound your whistle before a throw-in. Sound it when there may be legitimate confusion as to whether or not the ball is in play (like when defensive players have their backs to you). Sound it before the throw-in that follows a timeout or intermission. Also sound it after substitutions (especially when the ball stays in the frontcourt). There is occasional confusion during substitutions and the whistle helps all know play is about to begin. If you're going to sound your whistle and a player is nearby, turn your head away from the player so you don't blow the whistle right in the player's ear.

Refrain from sounding the whistle on all throw-ins though. Many times it is unnecessary and only draws more attention to the official. Use it sparingly and it will be appreciated.

Administering a Throw-in (5-4)

On all throw-ins, the officials use the boxing-in method. On all frontcourt endline throw-ins, the lead is positioned outside the thrower between the thrower and the sideline.

Officials may bounce or hand the ball to the thrower. The bounce to the thrower-in should only occur from the sideline or the backcourt endline.

To ensure proper court coverage when handing the ball to the thrower, use the inside hand. Before handing or bouncing the ball to the thrower, tell the players to ball is about to become live with short commands, like "ready" or "play it." That gives all players a fair start. Then the administering official must move away from the thrower. Staying too close to the thrower obscures court vision. Move for proper angles to avoid straightlining. Take at least one step laterally away from the thrower so your field of vision increases. You should also step back from the endline or sideline,

5-4A

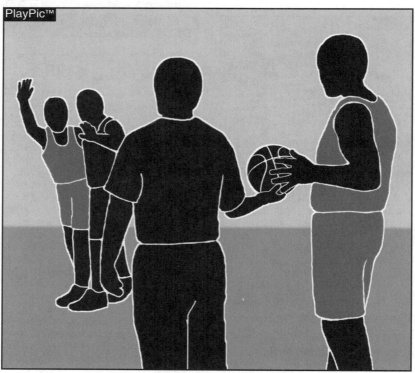

PlayPic™

increasing visual clearance and assuring proper perspective.

For the lead official, post play on throw-ins is often physical as players jockey for inside position and set screens to free teammates. The lead must see potential infractions by the thrower, potential infractions or fouls by the player defending the thrower and action nearest the throw-in.

In PlayPic 5-4A, the official hands the ball to the thrower with the hand closest to the thrower. In PlayPic 5-4B, the official steps away from the thrower and begins

the throw-in count. The count is silent.

The step away from the thrower allows the official to see the thrower and provides a better angle on the players jockeying for position. □

Throw-in Below Free-throw Line Extended (5-5)

The lead has primary on-ball coverage when the ball is below the free-throw line extended opposite the trail. When a throw-in occurs

5-4B

on the sideline opposite the trail below the free-throw line extended, the lead administers the throw-in using the boxing-in method by bouncing the ball to the thrower.

The adjustments means the lead and trail will not have to switch or move across the court to administer a throw-in below the free-throw line extended, a necessary practice in previous seasons.

In order for the lead to administer the sideline throw-in, significant coverage adjustments must be made. The lead must move closer toward the sideline before bouncing the ball to the thrower to

ensure a proper visual field that includes the thrower and throw-in plane. The lead should also get deep (move back away from the endline) to increase the field of vision and see secondary coverage of post play on the low block (MechaniGram 5-5).

With the lead focused nearer the throw-in, the trail must move off the opposite sideline and onto the court to officiate all off-ball action, including action in the lane area. The trail must be aggressive if an off-ball foul in the lane is detected, moving toward the foul to close the distance.

As with all throw-ins, the lead

5-5

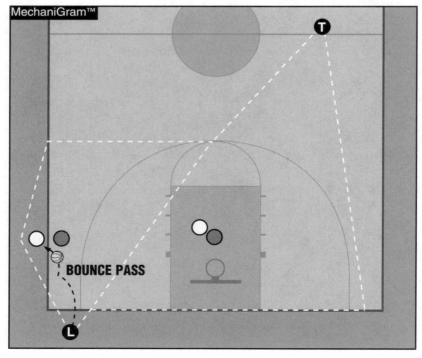

MechaniGram™

BOUNCE PASS

and trail should make eye contact before the lead bounces the ball to the thrower.

Keep in mind the lead administers throw-ins below the free-throw line extended *when the ball goes out of bounds on the lead's side of the court*. If the ball goes out of bounds below the free-throw line extended on the trail's side of the court (opposite the lead), the trail administers that throw-in. There's no need for the lead to come across the court to administer that throw-in because the trail would also have to cross the court to apply boxing-in principles.

Throw-ins: Boxing-in Method When Lead Administers (5-6)

The lead administers all throw-ins on the frontcourt endline. The thrower is always between the lead and the thrower's goal. The trail is positioned between the free-throw line extended and the division line, opposite the lead, to ensure both sidelines, both endlines and the division line are covered. □

5-6

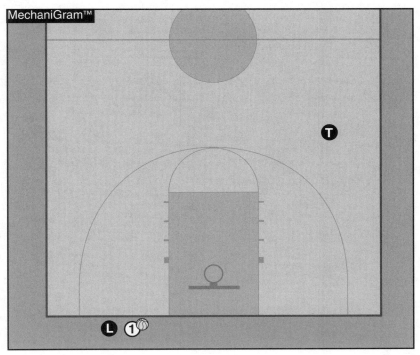

MechaniGram™

6 Transitions

Transition plays occur any time the ball moves from one end of the court to the other. On transition plays, the officials switch designations — from trail to lead and vice versa.

> The lead **"bumps" the trail down court** and the trail moving to lead "runs" the floor.

> The bump-and-run cuts the distance each official travels and gets the game going smoothly, allowing the crew to **establish and maintain a quality tempo.**

> The **same pass/crash principles** that apply in the lane area apply all over the court.

> When quick, long passes advance the ball upcourt, the new lead must be prepared to **help the trail** determine whether or not a shot is a three-point try.

> On some fastbreak plays, the trail moving to new lead can improve an angle on a play nearer the opposite sideline by **cutting the corner** while moving into the frontcourt.

> There are times when **officials get beat downcourt** on fastbreaks. That's OK.

> **Staying even with the players is about the *worst* thing** you can do for your angles.

CHECK LIST

✔ Wait and watch

✔ Stay open to the court

✔ Be ready to help

✔ It's OK to get beat

Keep your head up while moving upcourt, as Paul Tuttle, Indianapolis, does here.

JIM WHITE

The 'Bump-and-Run' (6-1)

The bump-and-run is a mechanic used by two-person crews to move swiftly from the frontcourt after a violation.

As the trail official, when an offensive violation occurs in your coverage area, stop the clock, signal the violation and the direction, then point to the spot for the throw-in. Next — after checking that there are no problems — sprint down court while viewing the action behind you and become the new lead official.

If you're the lead, eye the trail's signals, move toward the spot for the throw-in and administer it. You have now become the new trail. The lead "bumps" the trail down court and the trail moving to lead "runs" the floor.

In MechaniGram 6-1, ① causes the ball to go out-of-bounds. The trail correctly stops the clock, signals a violation and the direction, then communicates the throw-in spot to the lead. The trail then moves down court and becomes the new lead.

The bump-and-run serves two main purposes: The trail official has a better chance of avoiding problems near the violation and the officials move into place quicker and get the ball live faster.

The bump-and-run cuts the distance each official travels and gets the game going smoothly, allowing the crew to establish and maintain a quality tempo. ☐

6-1

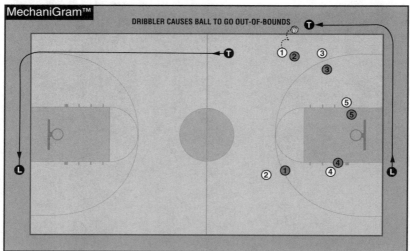

MechaniGram™

DRIBBLER CAUSES BALL TO GO OUT-OF-BOUNDS

Pass/crash Transition (6-2)

The same pass/crash principles that apply in the lane area apply all over the court. One trouble spot for officials is the pass/crash when a team in transition starts a break up the court. Many times you'll see players leave their feet to make a pass then crash into defenders. Block? Charge? No-call?

In MechaniGram 6-2, ④ rebounds and throws an outlet pass to a streaking ① . ① catches the pass and dribbles up court trying to start a fastbreak. ③ is filling the passing lane down the center of the court.

② steps in to stop ① from advancing into the frontcourt. ① leaps into the air and passes to ③ then crashes into ② .

The lead must quickly read the fastbreak and move toward the sideline to become the new trail. There the new trail has a good look at ① leaping, passing and crashing.

The trail who became the new lead must also quickly read the

6-2

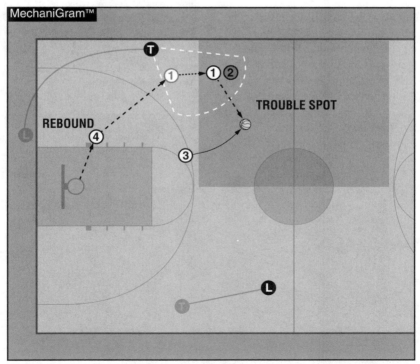

fastbreak and move into the front-court. The new lead's primary responsibility is ③ catching the pass. In rare circumstances, if the new trail did not get out on the break fast enough to see the crash, the new lead's secondary coverage area is the crash. That is more likely, however, when the pass/crash occurs in the center of the court. □

Lead Helps on Three-point Attempt (6-3)

The transition game is difficult to cover with a crew of two officials. It's especially tough when quick outlet passes lead to quick shots at the other end of the court.

When quick, long passes advance the ball upcourt, the new

lead must be prepared to help the trail determine whether or not a shot is a three-point try. The help occurs even though the shot attempt is in an area not normally covered by the lead. Why help?

Three-point attempt

6-3

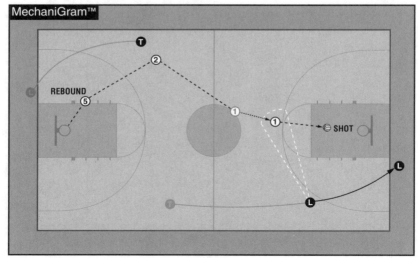

When there's a quick outlet pass that leads to another quick, long pass, the new trail usually doesn't have enough time to get into the frontcourt and get a good angle on a shot. Because of the distance and poor angle between the trail and the shot, the trail is left guessing.

The new lead must recognize the quick transition play and help the new trail by judging the shot.

In MechaniGram 6-3, ⑤ grabs the rebound and throws a quick, long outlet pass to ② , who throws another quick, long pass to ① .

① catches the pass near the center restraining circle, dribbles to the top of the key and shoots. The lead moving to new trail doesn't have enough time to get a good look at the shot. The trail moving to new lead recognizes that and makes the judgment on the shot, even though a top-of-the-key shot is normally covered by the trail.

When that type of transition play occurs near the end of a period, the new lead judges whether or not the shot was a three-pointer, but the trail still judges whether the shot was released in time — unless alternate coverage was previously discussed.

Lead Cuts Corner (6-4)

The benefits of good angles on transition plays are no different than getting good angles on any other play. Sometimes, because of the speed of the players, long outlet passes, etc., it is difficult to get a good angle on a transition play.

On some fastbreak plays, the trail moving to new lead can improve an angle on a play nearer the opposite sideline by cutting the corner while moving into the frontcourt. That can only happen effectively if (1) the new lead is

TOM IMPERIAL

well-ahead of — and can *stay* ahead of — the drive to the basket and (2) there are no other players in the area filling the passing lanes. If (1) and (2) are not in effect, remain closer to the near sideline and consider buttonhooking on the play.

If (1) and (2) are in effect, begin cutting the corner as you cross the free-throw line extended. Take a sharp angle under the basket to the far lane line. Keep your head up and watch the oncoming players at all times.

In MechaniGram 6-4, ① with defensive pressure dribbles from the backcourt to the frontcourt and is driving in for a layup. The trail moving to new lead stays well ahead of the play and there are no other players in the area filling passing lanes. The new lead cuts the corner at the free-throw line extended and moves to the far lane line to judge the play. The improved angle is similar to the ball-side look during a halfcourt play.

It takes anticipation and speed to cut the corner on a fastbreak play, but the reward is an improved angle that defeats straightlining. □

6-4

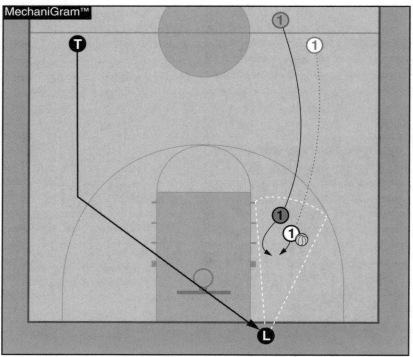

The Buttonhook (6-5)

There are times when officials get beat downcourt on fastbreaks. That's OK. In fact, if you're so worried about not getting beat you're probably leaving the lead official hanging alone with all the rebounding action — a definite no-no.

When you do get beat downcourt, there's no need to panic. There's a simple movement — the buttonhook — that can eliminate straightlining and allow you to officiate the play properly from behind. (It's called the buttonhook because the movement is similar to a football wide receiver's movement on a buttonhook pass pattern.)

Too often, an official who is trailing a fastbreak sprints as fast as possible (sometimes with their heads down) to stay even with the players. *Staying even with the players is about the worst thing you can do for your angles.* Either get ahead of the play and let it come comfortably to you (unlikely, unless you're a world-class sprint-

6-5A

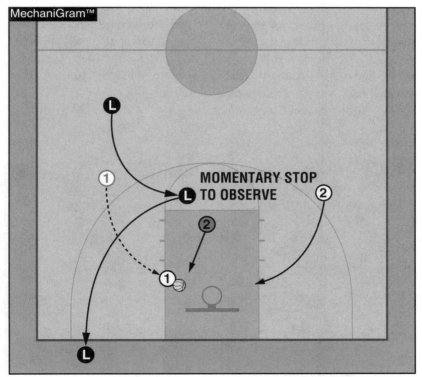

MechaniGram™

MOMENTARY STOP TO OBSERVE

er) or let it go and momentarily officiate the play from behind, as in MechaniGram 6-5A. Staying even means you're looking through bodies and guessing.

When officiating a play from behind, swing toward the middle of the court, roughly at the intersection of the lane line and the free-throw line. Momentarily pause there to watch the action (referee the defense). That movement allows you a good angle to observe potential contact. When that part of the play is over, swing back out toward the sideline and endline to get into proper position.

Be aware of players coming from behind you. You should be well ahead of the second wave of players coming down court. They'll see you in the middle of the court and avoid contact. Make sure your position in the center of the court is momentary; you want to move out of there before the second wave comes down. If you feel pressure from players behind you, think safety first. Stay there a bit longer if you have to to let players go by before you move to the endline.

In PlayPic 6-5B, the trail moving to new lead is behind the play and unable to get ahead of it. In PlayPic 6-5C, the new lead moves toward the middle of the court, roughly at the intersection of the lane line and the free-throw line, to officiate the play. After momentarily stopping to view the play, the lead moves back out toward the sideline and endline to get into proper position.

The buttonhook is a quick, simple movement that will eliminate the guesswork when trailing a play. It will help you get good angles. □

6-5B

6-5C

Court Coverage: Backcourt, Defensive Pressure (6-6)

When play moves from one endline toward the other, the trail has primary responsibility in the backcourt. However, when there's defensive pressure in the backcourt, sometimes the lead must help.

There is a general rule when the lead helps the trail in the backcourt. If there are four or fewer players in the backcourt, the trail works alone there. More than four players, the lead helps.

When there's more than four players in the backcourt, the lead is positioned near the division line. If all the players are in the backcourt, the lead may move closer to the backcourt endline for better angles. If some players are in the frontcourt, however, the division-line area is the best position.

When near the division line, the lead must stay wide and constantly glance from backcourt to frontcourt. That "swivel" glance allows the lead to help the trail with backcourt traffic plus watch players in the frontcourt. □

6-6

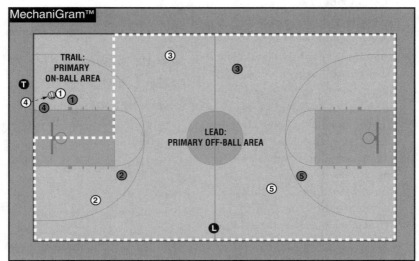

10 Ways to Louse Up a Game

By John Katzler

(Editor's note: The following is excerpted from Tip Off, *one of Referee's best-selling basketball officiating books. The book, published in 1986, is no longer in print but its content still applies today. Portions have been edited.)*

While the "perfect" game has rarely been worked by an official, that doesn't mean you should stop striving to reach that goal each and every time you step out onto the basketball floor. The following are 10 sure-fire ways for you to ruin the possibility of attaining your goal.

1. Whenever it looks like traveling, call it.

Have you heard that and blown the whistle for a traveling call? I'm referring to the situation in which a player muffs a pass or taps a rebound into the air more than once. He obviously moves anywhere from five to 10 feet or more during that action. However, he has not committed a violation. The key is to remember that traveling cannot occur without player control.

2. When you are administering a throw-in, rush the ball into play before your partner has indicated he is ready.

Although you want to keep the game moving, don't try to hedge in that situation. By hurrying a throw-in, you can catch both the players and your partner out of position, as well as fail to recognize a legal substitution. Always check the position of your partner before handing the ball on a throw-in. Use of proper mechanics will allow you to avoid the above pitfalls and bring desired calmness to the overall contest.

3. Call things differently later in the game from the way you did in the first half.

As in most any sport, rhythm, timing or tempo is a required part of officiating. Accordingly, each official must work on establishing that game tempo from the opening toss.

Consistency from the start is a must. Allowing excessive physical play in the early stages of a game and then tightening up toward the end is a good way to get into trouble and let the game get out of hand. All that can be avoided by setting your pattern early and following that path consistently throughout the game.

4. Start the game with a poorly thrown jump ball.

Without a doubt, that is one of the biggest faults of officials who work all levels of play. An easy way to avoid that is to simply practice tossing the ball. I've found that an investment of 10 minutes a day for about a week before the season begins will pay big dividends. Some basic elements of a good toss are: (a) Keep your weight forward; (b) Follow through with your arm(s); (c) Start the toss at least from chest level but not as high as eye level; (d) Concentrate on tossing the ball straight, high and with vigor so that neither jumper can steal the toss, and so the ball comes down to the same spot from which it started.

5. When a period- or game-ending horn sounds while the ball is in flight on a tap or field-goal attempt, wait until the horn sounds before signaling whether the bucket, if made, is good or not.

That is not the time to leave the coaches, players and crowd in suspense. Good mechanics dictate that the trail official (or sometimes the center official in three-person mechanics) should give the appropriate signal while the ball is in flight. If the shot was taken too late, the play should be wiped off immediately. If the shot was released in time, the official should extend his arm straight up into the air while indicating two (or three) points will score if the bucket goes. If the ball then goes into the bucket, the windmill arm motion follows.

6. Don't blow your whistle too loudly, someone might hear it.

The easiest way to get run out of the gym and officiating is to blow a weak whistle. If the situation calls for a whistle, blow it with authority. Just remember, a weak whistle almost always suggests that the official is in doubt. Don't appear uncertain for the lack of a little wind.

7. Whenever you assess a technical foul to a player or coach, stick the T sign right in his face.

When slapping a technical foul on a player or coach, the penalty is severe enough without rubbing salt in the wound. If there are any unwritten rules to follow in administering technicals, it's certain they include these mechanics: (a) Avoid rushing up to the offender, waving a guilty finger and shouting something like, "And that's number one!" Instead, maintain your floor position, give the proper signal and a firm but calm verbal communication of the infraction; (b) Handle the free throw(s) if you called the T; and (c) Let the other official administer the throw-in at midcourt, prefer-

ably at the side opposite the offending team's bench.

8. Whistle a held ball as quickly as possible, even if you're not sure the ball is tied up.

That is a common mistake; premature calling of a held ball should be avoided. Three key situations come to mind: (a) While A1 is holding the ball, B1 reaches in and merely touches the ball for a moment or two; (b) During a loose-ball situation, several opponents dive after the ball in an attempt to gain control. In the process, there is some incidental contact and it doesn't look too good; (c) During a field-goal attempt, B1 blocks the ball after it has traveled only a couple of inches from the shooter's hand and the ball is then caught by the shooter, who returns to the floor. In all of those cases nothing has occurred to cause a held ball. The main criterion that applies here is that opponents did not have their hands so firmly on the ball that control could not be obtained without undue roughness. Moral: Don't call a held ball just because "it looks bad" or to avoid trouble.

9. Whenever the ball is pinned against the backboard, whistle an infraction.

While in the NBA it is goaltending whenever a team B player pins against the backboard the shot of a team A player, that is not always the case at other levels of play; sometimes it is perfectly legal and other times a violation. Why the difference? If the ball is pinned on its upward flight and it is outside the basket cylinder and/or not on the rim, it is simply a blocked shot. However, if it's pinned on its downward flight outside the cylinder and not touching the rim but with a chance to score, then it is clearly a goaltending violation.

10. When the coach does something that clearly warrants a technical foul, pretend you don't see him and show everybody how you lack intestinal fortitude.

All of the prior material dealt with mechanics and rules. Now it's time for a little philosophy. Much is written each year about bench decorum and how, in general, officials fall down on the job of properly enforcing it. In spite of what the rulebook says a coach can or cannot do, the key to the whole situation is contained in one small word: guts. No matter how you slice it, coaches will go only as far as you let them. So do yourself a favor and let them know early in the game and in a proper manner who's in charge. That is not to suggest any vindictiveness, but merely not allowing the coaches to violate the spirit and intent of the rules.

(John Katzler, Mt. Prospect, Ill., refereed various levels of basketball for nearly four decades.) □

8 Postgame Review

After the game, it's a good idea to review what happened during the game. The postgame review is another important part of the learning process.

The first order of business immediately after the game is to relax. Officiating can be stressful and postgame relaxation helps get you back to normal.

At a reasonable time after the game, review the game with your partner. Some like to review before taking a shower and relaxing. Others like to wait until the postgame dinner. Do whatever is convenient and comfortable for you and your partner.

When reviewing the game, talk about:

Points of Emphasis

Were the pregame points of emphasis handled effectively. Many times, rough play is emphasized. Did you control the game effectively? Were off-ball fouls called appropriately? If the points of emphasis were not handled properly, discuss remedies for your next game.

Tempo

Did you let the game come to you or did you assert yourself when you didn't need to? Did the game develop a flow? If not, is there anything you could have done to keep the game moving? Did you get the ball back in play quickly without rushing?

Bench Decorum

How did you handle the benches? Did you let the coaches go too far? Were you approachable?

Strange Plays, Rulings

Discuss and review any strange plays or rulings. If necessary, confirm your ruling with the rulebook and casebook. Make sure you've got the rule down so you can apply it correctly if it happens again.

Solicit Constructive Criticism

One of the ways to improve is to get opinions and advice from others. Your partner is a great source. Always ask if there's anything you could have done differently or better.

After asking, accept the constructive criticism. Don't be one of those referees that asks, "How'd I do?" expecting a shower of praise. If you don't want to know the truth, don't ask. Take the criticism offered, analyze the comments and apply the changes if you feel it's appropriate.

Be ready to offer a critique when asked. It's frustrating for an official who wants to learn to invite criticism only to hear, "You did a good job." There must be something that needs improving! You ought to be able to give your partner at least three things to think about after every game.

Write a Journal

Consider keeping a journal during your season. Write down strange plays, your feelings about your performance, notes about your partner, things you did well and things you can improve on. The journal is a great way to look back during and after the season to see if there are patterns. If the same things keep appearing in your journal, you know there are things that need to be addressed.

Reviewing the journal is also a great way to start thinking about officiating before next season. □

The National Association of Sports Officials

- NASO's "Members Only Edition" of *Referee* magazine every month. Members receive 96-pages of *Referee* with 16-pages of association news, "members only" tips, case plays and ducational product discounts.

- Members receive a *FREE* educational publication valued up to $9.95.

- Discounts on NASO/*Referee* publications such as the Officials' Guidebooks, rules comparisons and sport-specific preseason publications make you a better official.

- Referral service in the event you move to another community.

- Web page and e-mail communications keep you updated on NASO news, services and benefits.

- "Ask Us" rules interpretations service.

- Sports-specific rules quizzes.

- Free NASO e-mail address.

- Free access to the *NASO LockerRoom* — an NASO cyberspace service.

- Membership Certificate and laminated membership card.

- NASO Code of Ethics.

For a complete brochure and membership information contact:
NASO • 2017 Lathrop Avenue • Racine, WI 53405
262/632-5448 • 262/632-5460 (fax)
naso@naso.org or visit our website at www.naso.org